Helen Steiner Rice

A
COLLECTION OF
BLESSINGS

VALUEBOOKS

An Imprint of Barbour Publishing, Inc.

A HELEN STEINER RICE ® Product

Print ISBN 978-1-63058-672-0

eBook editions:
Adobe Digital Edition (.epub) 978-1-63409-158-9
Kindle and MobiPocket Edition (.prc) 978-1-63409-159-6

The poetry of Helen Steiner Rice is published under
a licensing agreement with the Helen Steiner Rice
Foundation.

Special thanks to Virginia J. Ruehlmann for her cooperation
and assistance in the development of this book.

Published by Value Books, an imprint of Barbour
Publishing, Inc., P.O. Box 719, Uhrichsville, Ohio 44683,
www.barbourbooks.com

*Our mission is to publish and distribute inspirational products
offering exceptional value and biblical encouragement to the
masses.*

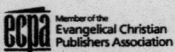 Member of the
Evangelical Christian
Publishers Association

Printed in the United States of America.

A NEW YEAR BRINGS
A NEW BEGINNING

As the New Year starts and the old year ends
There's no better time to make amends
For all the things we sincerely regret
And wish in our hearts we could somehow forget—
We all make mistakes, for it's human to err,
But no one need ever give up in despair,
For God gives us all a brand-new beginning,
A chance to start over and repent of our sinning—
And when God forgives us we, too, must forgive
And resolve to do better each day that we live
By constantly trying to be like Him more nearly
And to trust in His wisdom
and love Him more dearly—
Assured that we're never out of His care
And we're always welcome to seek Him in prayer.

A New Year!
A New Day!
A New Life!

Not only on New Year's but all the year through
God gives us a chance to begin life anew,
For each day at dawning we have but to pray
That all the mistakes that we made yesterday
Will be blotted out and forgiven by grace,
For God in His love will completely efface
All that is past and He'll grant a new start
To all who are truly repentant at heart.

THE HOPE OF THE WORLD

An empty tomb. . .a stone rolled away
Speak of the Savior who rose Easter Day. . .
But that was centuries and centuries ago,
And we ask today, Was it really so?
Did He walk on earth and live and die
And return to His Father to dwell on high?
We were not there to hear or see,
But our hopes and dreams of eternity
Are all centered on the Easter story
When Christ ascended and rose in glory. . .
And life on earth has not been the same,
Regardless of what the skeptics claim. . .
For, after the Lord was crucified,
Even the ones who had scoffed and denied
Knew that something had taken place
That nothing could ever remove or erase. . .
For hope was born in the soul of man,
And faith to believe in God's master plan
Stirred in the hearts to dispel doubt and fear,
And that faith has grown with each passing year. . .
For the hope of man is the Easter story.
For life is robbed of all meaning and glory
Unless man knows that he has a goal
And a resting place for his searching soul.

KEEP US GRATEFUL

Peace dawns once more on a war-torn earth,
While a world gone wild with hysteria and mirth
Raises its voice in loud jubilation
To try to express its heart's exultation.
Cities and towns and country places
Become a seething sea of faces.
Prayers, thanksgiving, and unchecked tears
Mingle with thunderous and unrestrained cheers.
Now in this hour of triumphal thanksgiving,
We pray for the dead and give thanks for the living.
May we never forget those who sleep 'neath the sod—
They helped liberate, by the grace of our God.
We've reached at long last the victor's goal,
But to keep the peace we must conquer the soul.
The struggle now enters a realm deep within,
And each man has his own private battle to win. . .
And the Unknown Soldier pleads to be heard,
And his message is told in Christ's stirring words,
"'Ye must be born again,' or we the slain
Have fought and fallen and died in vain."
Keep us grateful, omnipotent God,
And aware of those sleeping beneath the sod.
Heal the wounds and be with us yet,
Lest we forget—lest we forget.

A THANKSGIVING DAY PRAYER

Faith of our fathers, renew us again
And make us a nation of God-fearing men
Seeking Thy guidance, Thy love, and Thy will,
for we are but pilgrims in search of Thee still. . .
And gathered together on Thanksgiving Day,
May we lift up our hearts and our hands as we pray
To thank You for blessings we so little merit,
And grant us Thy love and teach us to share it.

A Birthday Is a Gateway

A birthday is a gateway
Between old years and new,
Just an opening to the future
Where we get a wider view.
For it takes a lot of birthdays
To make us wise and kind
And to help us judge all people
With our heart and not our mind.
Every year brings new dimensions
That enable us to see
All things within a kinder light
And more perceptively.
So birthdays are the gateway
To what the future holds
And to greater understanding
As the story of life unfolds.

SPRINGTIME GLORY

Flowers buried beneath the snow
Awakening again to live and grow—
Leaves that fell to the earth to die
Enriching the soil in which they lie—
Lifeless-looking, stark, stripped trees
Bursting with buds in the springtime breeze
Are just a few examples of
The greatness of God's power and love,
And in this blaze of springtime glory,
Just who could doubt the Easter story!

DAILY INSPIRATION

Special poems for special seasons
are meaningful indeed,
But daily inspiration is still man's greatest need.
For day by day all through the year,
not just on holidays,
Man should glorify the Lord in
deeds and words of praise.
And when the heart is heavy and
everything goes wrong,
May these daily words for daily needs
be like a cheery song
Assuring you He loves you and
that you never walk alone,
For in God's all-wise wisdom
your every need is known!

SHOWERS OF BLESSINGS

Each day there are showers of
blessings sent from the Father above,
For God is a great, lavish giver,
and there is no end to His love. . .
And His grace is more than sufficient,
His mercy is boundless and deep,
And His infinite blessings are countless—
and all this we're given to keep
If we but seek God and find Him
and ask for a bounteous measure
Of this wholly immeasurable offering
from God's inexhaustible treasure. . .
For no matter how big man's dreams are,
God's blessings are infinitely more,
For always God's giving is greater
than what man is asking for.

THE BLESSINGS OF
PATIENCE AND COMFORT

Realizing my helplessness,
I'm asking God if He will bless
The thoughts you think and all you do
So these dark hours you're passing through
Will lose their grave anxiety
And only deep tranquility
Will fill your mind and help impart
New strength and courage to your heart.
So take the Savior's loving hand
And do not try to understand—
Just let Him lead you where He will,
Through pastures green and waters still,
And though the way ahead seems steep,
Be not afraid for He will keep
Tender watch through night and day,
And He will hear each prayer you pray.

BLESSINGS DEVISED BY GOD

God speaks to us in many ways,
Altering our lives, our plans, and our days,
And His blessings come in many guises
That He alone in love devises,
And sorrow, which we dread so much,
Can bring a very healing touch. . .
For when we fail to heed His voice
We leave the Lord no other choice
Except to use a firm, stern hand
To make us know He's in command. . .
For on the wings of loss and pain,
The peace we often sought in vain
Will come to us with sweet surprise,
For God is merciful and wise. . .
And through dark hours of tribulation
God gives us time for meditation,
And nothing can be counted loss
Which teaches us to bear our cross.

NOT BY CHANCE OR
HAPPENSTANCE

Into our lives come many things
to break the dull routine—
The things we had not planned
or that happen unforeseen—
The sudden, unplanned meeting that
comes with sweet surprise
And lights the heart with happiness
like a rainbow in the skies.
Now some folks call it fickle fate
and some folks call it chance,
While others just accept it
as a pleasant happenstance.
But no matter what you call it,
it didn't come without design,
For all our lives are fashioned
by the hand that is divine
And every lucky happening and every lucky break
Are little gifts from God above
that are ours to freely take.

THINGS TO BE THANKFUL FOR

The good, green earth beneath our feet,
The air we breathe, the food we eat,
Some work to do, a goal to win,
A hidden longing deep within
That spurs us on to bigger things
And helps us meet what each day brings—
All these things and many more
Are things we should be thankful for. . .
And most of all, our thankful prayers
Should rise to God because He cares.

BLESSINGS IN DISGUISE

God sends His little angels in
many forms and guises.
They come as lovely miracles
that God alone devises,
For He does nothing without purpose—
everything's a perfect plan
To fulfill in bounteous measure
all He ever promised man. . .
For every little angel with a body bent or broken
Or a little mind challenged or little words unspoken
Is just God's way of trying to reach
out and touch the hands
Of all who do not know Him
and cannot understand
That often through an angel
whose wings will never fly
The Lord is pointing out the way to His eternal sky,
Where there will be no handicaps
of body, soul, or mind
And where all limitations will be
dropped and left behind. . .
So accept these little angels
as gifts from God above,
And thank Him for this lesson
in faith and hope and love.

BEYOND OUR ASKING

More than hearts can imagine
or minds comprehend,
God's bountiful gifts are ours without end.
We ask for a cupful when the vast sea is ours,
We pick a small rosebud from a garden of flowers,
We reach for a sunbeam but the sun still abides,
We draw one short breath but
there's air on all sides.
Whatever we ask for falls short of God's giving,
For His greatness exceeds every facet of living,
And always God's ready and eager and willing
To pour out His mercy, completely fulfilling
All of man's needs for peace, joy, and rest,
For God gives His children whatever is best.
Just give Him a chance to open His treasures,
And He'll fill your life with
unfathomable pleasures—
Pleasures that never grow worn out and faded
And leave us depleted, disillusioned, and jaded—
For God has a storehouse just filled to the brim
With all that man needs, if we'll only ask Him.

A SURE WAY TO A HAPPY DAY

Happiness is something we create in our minds—
It's not something you search for
And so seldom find.
It's just waking up and beginning the day
By counting our blessings and kneeling to pray.
It's giving up thoughts that breed discontent
And accepting what comes as a gift heaven-sent.
It's giving up wishing for things we have not
And making the best of whatever we've got.
It's knowing that life is determined for us
And pursuing our tasks
Without fret, fume, or fuss. . .
For it's by completing what God gives us to do
That we find real contentment and happiness, too.

A Thankful Heart

Take nothing for granted, for whenever you do,
The joy of enjoying is lessened for you.
For we rob our own lives much more than we know
when we fail to respond or in any way show
Our thanks for the blessings that daily are ours—
The warmth of the sun, the fragrance of flowers,
The beauty of twilight, the freshness of dawn,
The coolness of dew on a green velvet lawn,
The kind little deeds so thoughtfully done,
The favors of friends and the love that someone
Unselfishly gives us in myriad ways,
Expecting no payment and no words of praise.
Oh, great is our loss when we no longer find
A thankful response to things of this kind.
For the joy of enjoying and the fullness of living
Are found in the heart
that is filled with thanksgiving.

Do Not Be Anxious

Do not be anxious, said our Lord,
Have peace from day to day—
The lilies neither toil nor spin,
Yet none are clothed as they.
The meadowlark with sweetest song
Fears not for bread or nest
Because he trusts our Father's love
And God knows what is best.

IN HOURS OF DISCOURAGEMENT, GOD IS OUR ENCOURAGEMENT

God has given us the answers,
which too often go unheeded,
But if we search His promises,
we'll find everything that's needed
To lift our faltering spirits and renew our courage, too,
For there's absolutely nothing too much for God to do. . .
For the Lord is our salvation and
our strength in every fight,
Our redeemer and protector, our eternal guiding light.
He has promised to sustain us,
He's our refuge from all harms,
And underneath this refuge are the everlasting arms. . .
So cast your burden on Him,
seek His counsel when distressed,
And go to Him for comfort when
you're lonely and oppressed. . .
For in God is our encouragement in trouble and in trials,
And in suffering and in sorrow He will
turn our tears to smiles.

NEVER BE DISCOURAGED

There is really nothing we need know
or even try to understand
If we refuse to be discouraged
and trust God's guiding hand,
So take heart and meet each minute
with faith in God's great love,
Aware that every day of life
is controlled by God above
And never dread tomorrow
or what the future brings
Just pray for strength and courage
and trust God in all things,
And never grow discouraged—
be patient and just wait,
For God never comes too early,
and He never comes too late.

No Room for Blessings

Refuse to be discouraged—
refuse to be distressed,
For when we are despondent,
our lives cannot be blessed.
Doubt and fear and worry close
the door to faith and prayer,
And there's no room for blessings
when we're lost in deep despair.
So remember when you're troubled
with uncertainty and doubt,
It is best to tell our Father
what our fear is all about.
For unless we seek His guidance
when troubled times arise,
We are bound to make decisions
that are twisted and unwise.
But when we view our problems
through the eyes of God above,
Misfortunes turn to blessings
and hatred turns to love.

BLESSINGS COME IN MANY GUISES

When troubles come and things go wrong
And days are cheerless and nights are long,
We find it so easy to give in to despair
By magnifying the burdens we bear.
We add to our worries by refusing to try
To look for the rainbow in an overcast sky,
And the blessings God sent in a darkened disguise
Our troubled hearts fail to recognize,
Not knowing God sent it not to distress us
But to strengthen our faith and redeem us and bless us.

GOD'S MESSENGERS

The unexpected kindness from an unexpected place,
A hand outstretched in friendship,
a smile on someone's face,
A word of understanding spoken in a time of trial
Are unexpected miracles
that make life more worthwhile.
We know not how it happened
that in an hour of need
Somebody out of nowhere
proved to be a friend indeed. . .
For God has many messengers we fail to recognize,
But He sends them when we need them,
and His ways are wondrous and wise. . .
So keep looking for an angel
and keep listening to hear,
For on life's busy, crowded streets,
you will find God's presence near.

THERE ARE BLESSINGS
IN EVERYTHING

Blessings come in many guises
That God alone in love devises,
And sickness, which we dread so much,
Can bring a very healing touch,
For often on the wings of pain
The peace we sought before in vain
Will come to us with sweet surprise,
For God is merciful and wise. . .
And through long hours of tribulation
God gives us time for meditation,
And no sickness can be counted loss
That teaches us to bear our cross.

LOOK ON THE SUNNY SIDE

There are always two sides—the good and the bad,
The dark and the light, the sad and the glad. . .
But in looking back over the good and the bad,
We're aware of the number
of good things we've had—
And in counting our blessings,
we find when we're through
We've no reason at all to complain or be blue. . .
So thank God for the good things
He has already done,
And be grateful to Him for
the battles you've won—
And know that the same God
who helped you before
Is ready and willing to help you once more—
Then with faith in your heart,
reach out for God's hand
And accept what He sends,
though you can't understand. . .
For our Father in heaven always knows what is best,
And if you trust His wisdom,
your life will be blessed. . .
For always remember that whatever betide you,
You are never alone, for God is beside you.

A RAINBOW OF HOPE

The rainbow is God's promise
of hope for you and me,
And though the clouds hang heavy
and the sun we cannot see,
We know above the dark clouds
that fill the stormy sky
Hope's rainbow will come shining through
when the clouds have drifted by.

IT'S A WONDERFUL WORLD

In spite of the fact we complain and lament
And view this old world with much discontent,
Deploring conditions and grumbling because
There's so much injustice and so many flaws,
It's a wonderful world, and it's people like you
Who make it that way by the things that they do.
For a warm, ready smile or a kind, thoughtful deed
Or a hand outstretched in an hour of need
Can change our whole outlook
and make the world bright
Where a minute before just nothing seemed right.
It's a wonderful world and it always will be
If we keep our eyes open and focused to see
The wonderful things we are capable of
When we open our hearts to God and His love.

GOD'S TENDER CARE

When trouble comes, as it does to us all
God is so great and we are so small—
But there is nothing that we need know
If we have faith that wherever we go
God will be waiting to help us bear
Our pain and sorrow, our suffering and care—
For no pain or suffering is ever too much
To yield itself to God's merciful touch!

There's Peace and Calm in the Twenty-third Psalm

With the Lord as your Shepherd
you have all that you need,
For if you follow in His footsteps
wherever He may lead,
He will guard and guide and keep you
in His loving, watchful care,
And when traveling in dark valleys,
your Shepherd will be there. . .
His goodness is unfailing,
His kindness knows no end,
For the Lord is a Good Shepherd
on whom you can depend. . .
So when your heart is troubled,
you'll find quiet, peace, and calm
If you'll open up the Bible and
just read this treasured psalm.

THERE IS A REASON
FOR EVERYTHING

God never hurts us needlessly
and He never wastes our pain;
For every loss He sends to us
is followed by rich gain.
And when we count the blessings
that God has so freely sent,
We will find no cause for murmuring
and no time to lament.
For our Father loves His children
and to Him all things are plain;
He never sends us pleasure when
the soul's deep need is pain.
So whenever we are troubled
and when everything goes wrong,
It is just God working in us
to make our spirits strong.

SOMEBODY CARES

Somebody cares and always will—
The world forgets, but God loves you still.
You cannot go beyond His love
No matter what you're guilty of,
For God forgives until the end—
He is your faithful, loyal friend. . .
And though you try to hide your face,
There is no shelter anyplace
That can escape His watchful eye,
For on the earth and in the sky
He's ever-present and always there
To take you in His tender care
And bind the wounds and mend the breaks
When all the world around forsakes.
Somebody cares and loves you still,
And God is the Someone who always will.

SOMEBODY LOVES YOU

Somebody loves you more than you know,
Somebody goes with you wherever you go,
Somebody really and truly cares
And lovingly listens to all of your prayers. . .
Don't doubt for a minute that this is not true,
For God loves His children
and takes care of them, too. . .
And all of His treasures are yours to share
If you love Him completely
and show that you care. . .
And if you walk in His footsteps
and have faith to believe,
There's nothing you ask for
that you will not receive!

GOD WILL NOT FAIL YOU

When life seems empty and there's no place to go,
When your heart is troubled
and your spirits are low,
When friends seem few and nobody cares—
There is always God to hear your prayers. . .
And whatever you're facing will seem much less
When you go to God and confide and confess,
For the burden that seems too heavy to bear
God lifts away on the wings of prayer. . .
And seen through God's eyes
earthly troubles diminish,
And we're given new strength to face and to finish
Life's daily tasks as they come along
If we pray for strength to keep us strong. . .
So go to our Father when troubles assail you,
For His grace is sufficient and He'll never fail you.

NEVER ALONE

Since fear and dread and worry
Cannot help in any way,
It's much healthier and happier
To be cheerful every day—
And if we'll only try it
We will find, without a doubt,
A cheerful attitude's something
No one should be without—
For when the heart is cheerful
It cannot be filled with fear,
And without fear the way ahead
Seems more distinct and clear—
And we realize there's nothing
We need ever face alone,
For our heavenly Father loves us
And our problems are His own.

EAGLES' WINGS

How little we know what God has in store
As daily He blesses our lives more and more.
I've lived many years and learned many things,
But today I have grown new spiritual wings,
For pain has a way of broadening our view
And bringing us closer in sympathy, too,
To those who are living in constant pain
And trying somehow to bravely sustain
The faith and endurance to keep on trying
When they'd almost welcome the peace of dying.
And without this experience
I would have lived and died
Without fathoming the pain of Christ crucified,
For none of us know what pain's all about
Until our spiritual wings start to sprout.
So thank You, God, for the gift You sent
To teach me that pain is heaven-sent.

BE GLAD

Be glad that your life has been full and complete,
Be glad that you've tasted the bitter and sweet.
Be glad that you've walked in sunshine and rain,
Be glad that you've felt both pleasure and pain.
Be glad that you've had such a full, happy life,
Be glad for your joy as well as your strife.
Be glad that you've walked with courage each day,
Be glad you've had strength for each step of the way.
Be glad for the comfort that you've found in prayer.
Be glad for God's blessings, His love, and His care.

COUNT YOUR GAINS,
NOT YOUR LOSSES

As we travel down life's busy road
Complaining of our heavy load,
We often think God's been unfair
And given us much more than our share
Of daily little irritations
And disappointing tribulations.
We're discontented with our lot
And all the bad breaks that we got.
We count our losses, not our gain,
And remember only tears and pain.
The good things we forget completely—
When God looked down and blessed us sweetly.
And so we walk with heads held low,
And little do we guess or know
That someone near us on life's street
Is burdened deeply with defeat,
And if we'd but forget our care
And stop in sympathy to share
The burden that our brother carried,
Our minds and hearts would be less harried
And we would feel our load was small—
In fact, we carried no load at all.

LOOK UP

It's easy to grow downhearted
when nothing goes your way,
It's easy to be discouraged
when you have a troublesome day,
But trouble is only a challenge
to spur you on to achieve
The best that God has to offer
if you have the faith to believe!

UNAWARE, WE PASS HIM BY

On life's busy thoroughfares
We meet with angels unawares,
But we are too busy to listen or hear,
Too busy to sense that God is near,
Too busy to stop and recognize
The grief that lies in another's eyes,
Too busy to offer to help or share,
Too busy to sympathize or care,
Too busy to do the good things we should,
Telling ourselves we would if we could. . .
But life is too swift and the pace is too great,
And we dare not pause, for we might be too late
For our next appointment, which means so much;
We are willing to brush off the Savior's touch.
And we tell ourselves there will come a day
When we'll have more time to pause on our way,
But before we know it, life's sun has set,
And we've passed the Savior but never met.
For hurrying along life's thoroughfare,
We passed Him by but remained unaware
That within the very sight of our eyes,
Unnoticed, the Son of God passed by.

NOT WHAT YOU WANT
BUT WHAT GOD WANTS

Do you want what you want when you want it?
Do you pray and expect a reply?
And when it's not instantly answered
Do you feel that God passed you by?
Well, prayers that are prayed in this manner
Are really not prayers at all,
For you can't go to God in a hurry
And expect Him to answer your call.
For prayers are not meant for obtaining
What we selfishly wish to acquire,
For God in His wisdom refuses
The things that we wrongly desire. . .
Wake up! You are missing completely
The reason and purpose of prayer,
Which is really to keep us contented
That God holds us safe in His care.
And God only answers our pleadings
When He knows that our wants fill a need,
And whenever our will becomes His will,
There is no prayer that God does not heed!

SEEK FIRST THE KINGDOM OF GOD

Life is mixture of sunshine and rain,
Good things and bad things, pleasure and pain.
We can't have all sunshine, but it's certainly true
That there's never a cloud the sun doesn't shine through. . .
So always remember, whatever betide you,
The power of God is always beside you. . .
For God is your Father and no one can bar
Or keep you from reaching your desired success
Or withhold the joy that is yours to possess. . .
For with God on your side, it matters not who
Is working to keep life's good things from you,
For you need nothing more than God's guidance and love
To ensure you the things that you're most worthy of. . .
So trust in His wisdom and follow His ways
And be not concerned with the world's empty praise,
But first seek His kingdom and you will possess
The world's greatest of riches, which is true happiness.

THE PEACE WE'RE SEEKING

If we but had the eyes to see
God's face in every cloud,
If we but had the ears to hear
His voice above the crowd;
If we could feel His gentle touch
In every springtime breeze
And find a haven in His arms
'Neath sheltering, leafy trees. . .
If we could just lift up our hearts
Like flowers to the sun
And trust His loving promise
And pray, "Thy will be done,"
We'd find the peace we're seeking,
The kind no man can give,
The peace that comes from knowing
He died so we might live!

FAITH, NOT FEELING

When everything is pleasant and bright
And the things we do turn out just right,
We feel without question that God is real,
For when we are happy, how good we feel. . .
But when the tides turn and gone is the song
And misfortune comes and our plans go wrong,
Doubt creeps in and we start to wonder,
And our thoughts about God are torn asunder—
For we feel deserted in time of deep stress,
Without God's presence to assure us and bless. . .
And it is then when our senses are reeling
We realize clearly it's faith and not feeling—
For it takes great faith to patiently wait,
Believing God comes not too soon or too late.

THREE TREASURES

There are three treasures
More priceless than gold.
For if you possess them
You've riches untold—
For with faith to believe
What your eyes cannot see,
And hope to look forward
To joy yet to be,
And love to transform
The most commonplace
Into beauty and kindness
And goodness and grace,
There's nothing too much
To accomplish or do.
For with faith, hope, and love
To carry you through,
Your life will be happy
And full and complete.
For with faith, hope, and love
The bitter turns sweet.

THE BLESSINGS OF GOD'S SEASONS

We know we must pass through the seasons God sends,
Content in the knowledge that everything ends,
And oh, what a blessing to know there are reasons
And to find that our souls must, too,
have their seasons—
Bounteous seasons and barren ones, too,
Times for rejoicing and times to be blue—
But meeting these seasons of dark desolation
With the strength that is born of anticipation
Comes from knowing that every season of sadness
Will surely be followed by a springtime of gladness.

THE AUTUMN OF LIFE

What a wonderful time is life's autumn,
when the leaves of the trees are all gold,
When God fills each day as He sends it
with memories, priceless and old,
What a treasure-house filled with rare jewels
are the blessings of year upon year,
When life has been lived as you've lived it
in a home where God's presence is near. . .
May the deep meaning surrounding this day,
like the paintbrush of God up above,
Touch your life with wonderful blessings
and fill your heart brimful with His love.

GROWING OLDER IS
PART OF GOD'S PLAN

You can't hold back the dawn
or stop the tides from flowing
Or keep a rose from withering
or still a wind that's blowing—
And time cannot be halted
in its swift and endless flight,
For age is sure to follow youth
like day comes after night. . .
For He who sets our span of years
and watches from above
Replaces youth and beauty
with peace and truth and love—
And then our souls are privileged
to see a hidden treasure
That in youth escapes our eyes
in our pursuit of pleasure. . .
So passing years are but blessings
that open up the way
To the everlasting beauty of God's eternal day.

LIFE'S GOLDEN AUTUMN

Memory opens wide the door on a happy day like this,
And with a sweet nostalgia we longingly recall
The happy days of long ago that seem the best of all. . .
But time cannot be halted
in its swift and endless flight,
And age is sure to follow youth
as day comes after night,
And once again it's proven
that the restless brain of man
Is powerless to alter God's great, unchanging plan. . .
But while our steps grow slower
and we grow more tired, too,
The soul goes roaring upward
to realms untouched and new,
Where God's children live forever
in the beauty of His love.

NEW LIFE

And in the resurrection
That takes place in nature's sod,
Let us understand more fully
The risen Son of God.
And let us see the beauty
And the glory and the grace
That surrounds us in the springtime
As the smiling of God's face.
And through a happy springtime
And a summer filled with love,
May we walk into the autumn
With our thoughts on God above:
The God who sends the winter
And wraps the earth in death
Will always send the springtime
With an awakening breath
To every flower and leaflet
And to every shrub and tree,
And that same God will also send
New life to you and me.

WITH HIM FOREVER

The waking earth in springtime
Reminds us it is true
That nothing really ever dies
That will not rise anew. . .
So trust God's all-wise wisdom
And doubt the Father never,
For in His heavenly Kingdom
You'll live with Him forever.

THE HAND OF GOD IS EVERYWHERE

It's true we have never looked on His face,
But His likeness shines forth from every place,
For the hand of God is everywhere
Along life's busy thoroughfare,
And His presence can be felt and seen
Right in the midst of our daily routine.
Things we touch and see and feel
Are what make God so very real.

"In Him We Live and Move and Have Our Being"

We walk in a world that is strange and unknown,
And in the midst of the crowd we still feel alone.
We question our purpose, our part, and our place
In this vast land of mystery suspended in space.
We probe and explore and try hard to explain
The tumult of thoughts that our minds entertain,
But all of our problems and complex explanations
Of man's inner feelings and fears and frustrations
Still leave us engulfed in the mystery of life
With all of its struggles and suffering and strife,
Unable to fathom what tomorrow will bring—
But there is one truth to which we can cling. . .
For while life's a mystery man can't understand,
The great Giver of life is holding our hands,
And safe in His care there is no need for seeing,
"For in Him we live and move and have our being."

MY GOD IS NO STRANGER

I've never seen God, but I know how I feel—
It's people like you who make Him so real.
My God is no stranger—He's so friendly each day,
And He doesn't ask me to weep when I pray.
It seems that I pass Him so often each day
In the faces of people I meet on my way.
He's the stars in the heavens, a smile on some face,
A leaf on a tree or a rose in a vase.
He's winter and autumn and summer and spring—
In short, God is every real, wonderful thing.
I wish I might meet Him much more than I do—
I wish that there were more people like you.

His Likeness Shines Forth

In everything both great and small
We see the hand of God in all,
And every day, somewhere, someplace,
We see the likeness of His face.
For who can watch a new day's birth
Or touch the warm, life-giving earth
Or feel the softness of a breeze
Or look at skies through lacy trees
And say they've never seen His face
Or looked upon His throne of grace.
And man's search for God will end and begin
When he opens his heart to let Christ in.

THE EARTH IS THE LORD'S

"The earth is the Lord's and the fullness thereof"—
It speaks of His greatness and it sings of His love.
Through all of creation with symphonic splendor,
God speaks with a voice that is gentle and tender.
And the birds in the trees and the flowers of spring
All join in proclaiming this heavenly King.

GOD SO LOVED THE WORLD

Our Father up in heaven, long, long years ago,
Looked down in His great mercy
upon the earth below
And saw that folks were lonely
and lost in deep despair,
And so He said, "I'll send My Son
to walk among them there
So they can hear Him speaking
and feel His nearness, too,
And see the many miracles that faith alone can do.
For I know it will be easier to
believe and understand
If man can see and talk to Him
and touch His healing hand."
So whenever we have troubles
and we're overcome by cares,
We can take it all to Jesus, for He
understands our prayers.

THE BETTER YOU KNOW HIM, THE MORE YOU LOVE HIM!

The better you know God, the better you feel,
For to learn more about Him and discover He's real
Can wholly, completely, and miraculously change,
Reshape and remake and then rearrange
Your mixed-up, miserable, and unhappy life
Adrift on the sea of sin-sickened strife—
But when you once know this Man of goodwill,
He will calm your life and say, "Peace, be still". . .
So open your heart's door and let Christ come in
And He'll give you new life and free you from sin—
And there is no joy that can ever compare
With the joy of knowing you're in God's care.

A Pattern for Living

"Love one another as I have loved you"
May seem impossible to do,
But if you will try to trust and believe,
Great are the joys that you will receive.
For love makes us patient, understanding, and kind,
And we judge with our hearts and not with our minds,
For as soon as love enters the heart's open door,
The faults we once saw are not there anymore—
And the things that seem wrong begin to look right
When viewed in the softness of love's gentle light
For love works in ways that are wondrous and strange,
And there is nothing in life that love cannot change,
And all that God promised will someday come true
When you love one another the way He loved you.

GOD LOVES US

We are all God's children
and He loves us, every one.
He freely and completely
forgives all that we have done,
Asking only if we're ready
to follow where He leads,
Content that in His wisdom
He will answer all our needs.

WHAT MORE CAN YOU ASK?

God's love endures forever—
what a wonderful thing to know
When the tides of life run against you
and your spirit is downcast and low.
God's kindness is ever around you,
always ready to freely impart
Strength to your faltering spirit,
cheer to your lonely heart.
God's presence is ever beside you,
as near as the reach of your hand.
You have but to tell Him your troubles—
there is nothing He won't understand. . .
And knowing God's love is unfailing,
and His mercy unending and great,
You have but to trust in His promise—
God comes not too soon or too late. . .
So wait with a heart that is patient
for the goodness of God to prevail,
For never do prayers go unanswered,
and His mercy and love never fail.

HE LOVES YOU

It's amazing and incredible,
but it's as true as it can be—
God loves and understand us all,
and that means you and me.
His grace is all-sufficient for
both the young and old,
For the lonely and the timid,
for the brash and for the bold.
His love knows no exceptions,
so never feel excluded—
No matter who or what you are,
your name has been included. . .
And no matter what your past has been,
trust God to understand,
And no matter what your problem is,
just place it in His hand. . .
For in all our unloveliness
this great God loves us still—
He loved us since the world began,
and what's more, He always will!

A Friend Is a Gift from God

Among the great and glorious gifts
our heavenly Father sends
Is the gift of understanding that
we find in loving friends. . .
For in this world of trouble
that is filled with anxious care,
Everybody needs a friend in
whom they're free to share
The little secret heartaches
that lay heavy on the mind—
Not just a mere acquaintance
but someone who's just our kind. . .
So when we need some sympathy
or a friendly hand to touch
Or one who listens and speaks
words that mean so much,
We seek a true and trusted friend
in the knowledge that we'll find
A heart that's sympathetic and
an understanding mind. . .
And often just without a word
there seems to be a union
Of thoughts and kindred feelings,
for God gives true friends communion.

THE GIFT OF FRIENDSHIP

Friendship is a priceless gift that
cannot be bought or sold
But its value is far greater than a
mountain made of gold—
For gold is cold and lifeless,
it can neither see nor hear,
And in the time of trouble it is powerless to cheer.
It has no ears to listen, no heart to understand,
It cannot bring you comfort
or reach out a helping hand—
So when you ask God for a gift,
be thankful if He sends
Not diamonds, pearls, or riches,
but the love of real true friends.

A GIFT OF LOVE

Time is not measured by the years that you live
But by the deeds that you do and the joy that you give...
And from birthday to birthday, the good Lord above
Bestows on His children the gift of His love,
Asking us only to share it with others
By treating all people not as strangers but brothers...
And each day as it comes brings a chance to each one
To live to the fullest, leaving nothing undone
That would brighten the life or lighten the load
Of some weary traveler lost on life's road...
So what does it matter how long we may live
If as long as we live we unselfishly give.

THE BLESSING OF SHARING

Only what we give away
Enriches us from day to day,
For not in getting but in giving
Is found the lasting joy of living,
For no one ever had a part
In sharing treasures of the heart
Who did not feel the impact of
The magic mystery of God's love.
Love alone can make us kind
And give us joy and peace of mind,
So live with joy unselfishly
And you'll be blessed abundantly.

HEART GIFTS

It's not the things that can be bought
That are life's richest treasures;
It's just the little "heart gifts"
That money cannot measure—
A cheerful smile, a friendly word,
A sympathetic nod,
All priceless little treasures
From the storehouse of our God—
They are the things that can't be bought
With silver or with gold,
For thoughtfulness and kindness
And love are never sold—
They are the priceless things in life
For which no one can pay,
And the giver finds rich recompense
In giving them away.

Give Lavishly! Live Abundantly!

The more you give, the more you get—
The more you laugh, the less you fret.
The more you do unselfishly,
The more you live abundantly—
The more of everything you share,
The more you'll always have to spare.
The more you love, the more you'll find
That life is good and friends are kind,
For only what we give away
Enriches us from day to day.

WINGS OF PRAYER

On the wings of prayer our burdens take flight
And our load of care becomes bearably light,
And our heavy hearts are lifted above
To be healed by the balm of God's wondrous love,
And the tears in our eyes are dried by the hands
Of a loving Father who understands
All of our problems, our fears and despair,
When we take them to Him on the wings of prayer.

FAITH TO MEET EACH TRIAL

From one day to another,
God will gladly give
To everyone who seeks Him
and tries each day to live
A little bit more closely
to God and to each other,
Seeing everyone who passes
as a neighbor, friend, or brother,
Not only joy and happiness
but the faith to meet each trial
Not with fear and trepidation
but with an inner smile.
For we know life's never measured by
how many years we live
But by the kindly things we do
and the happiness we give.

WHAT IS PRAYER?

Is it measured words that are memorized,
Forcefully said and dramatized,
Offered with pomp and with arrogant pride
In words unmatched to the feelings inside?
No, prayer is so often just words unspoken,
Whispered in tears by a heart that is broken,
For God is already deeply aware
Of the burdens we find too heavy to bear. . .
And all we need do is seek Him in prayer
And without a word He will help us to bear
Our trials and troubles, our sickness and sorrow
And show us the way to a brighter tomorrow.
There's no need at all for impressive prayer,
For the minute we seek God, He's already there.

THE HOUSE OF PRAYER

Just close your eyes and open your heart
And feel your cares and worries depart.
Just yield yourself to the Father above
And let Him hold you secure in His love. . .
For life on earth grows more involved
With endless problems that can't be solved,
But God only asks us to do our best—
Then He will take over and finish the rest. . .
So when you are tired, discouraged, and blue,
There's always one door that is opened to you
And that is the door to the house of prayer,
And you'll find God waiting to meet you there. . .
And the house of prayer is no farther away
Than the quiet spot where you kneel and pray.
For the heart is a temple when God is there
As we place ourselves in His loving care. . .
And He hears every prayer and answers each one
When we pray in His name, "Thy will be done."
And the burdens that seemed too heavy to bear
Are lifted away on the wings of prayer.

THOUGHTS OF PEACE

Whenever I am troubled and lost in deep despair
I bundle all my troubles up
and go to God in prayer. . .
I tell Him I am heartsick and lost and lonely, too,
That my heart is deeply burdened
and I don't know what to do. . .
But I know He stilled the tempest
and calmed the angry sea,
And I humbly ask if in His love
He'll do the same for me. . .
And then I just keep quiet
and think only thoughts of peace,
And if I abide in stillness
my restless murmurings cease.

TALK IT OVER WITH GOD

You're worried and troubled about everything,
Wondering and fearing what tomorrow will bring.
You long to tell someone, for you feel so alone,
But your friends are all burdened
with cares of their own.
There is only one place and only one friend
Who is never too busy, and you can always depend
On Him to be waiting with arms open wide
To hear all the troubles you came to confide. . .
For the heavenly Father will always be there
When you seek Him and find Him
at the altar of prayer.

Daily Prayers Dissolve
Your Cares

We all have cares and problems we cannot solve alone,
But if we go to God in prayer,
we are never on our own,
And if we try to stand alone,
we are weak and we will fall,
For God is always greatest
when we're helpless, lost, and small. . .
And no day is unmeetable
if on rising, our first thought
Is to thank God for the blessings
that His loving care has brought,
So meet Him in the morning and
go with Him through the day
And thank Him for His guidance
each evening when you pray—
And if you follow faithfully this daily way to pray,
You will never in your lifetime
face another hopeless day. . .
For like a soaring eagle, you, too, can rise above
The storms of life around you
on the wings of prayer and love.

NO PRAYER GOES UNHEARD

Often we pause and wonder
when we kneel down and pray,
Can God really hear the prayers that we say?
But if we keep praying and talking to Him,
He'll brighten the soul that was clouded and dim,
And as we continue, our burden seems lighter,
Our sorrow is softened, and our outlook is brighter.
For though we feel helpless
and alone when we start,
A prayer is the key that opens the heart,
And as the heart opens, the dear Lord comes in.
And the prayer that we felt we could never begin
Is so easy to say, for the Lord understands
And He gives us new strength
by the touch of His hands.

RENEWAL

When life has lost its luster
and it's filled with dull routine,
When you long to run away from it,
seeking pastures new and green,
Remember, no one runs away from life
without finding when they do
So when your heart is heavy
and your day is dull with care,
Instead of trying to escape,
why not withdraw in prayer?
For in prayer there is renewal
of the spirit, mind, and heart,
For everything is lifted up
in which God has a part—
For when we go to God in prayer,
our thoughts are rearranged,
So even though our problems
have not been solved or changed,
Somehow the good Lord gives us
the power to understand
That He who holds tomorrow
is the One who holds our hands.

HEART SONG

There are so many, many times
God seems so far away
That I can't help but wonder
if He hears me when I pray.
Then I beseech Him earnestly
to hear my humble plea
And tell me how to serve Him
and to do it gallantly. . .
And so I pray this little prayer
and hope that He will show me
How I can bring more happiness
to all the folks who know me—
And give me hope and courage,
enough for every day,
And faith to light the darkness
when I stumble on my way,
And love and understanding,
enough to make me kind,
So I may judge all people
with my heart and not my mind.

GOD ALREADY KNOWS

Beyond that which words can interpret
or theology can explain
The world feels a shower of refreshment
that falls like the gentle rain
On hearts that are parched with problems
and are searching to find the way
To somehow attract God's attention
through well-chosen words as they pray,
Not knowing that God in His wisdom
can sense all man's worry and woe,
For there is nothing man can conceal
that God does not already know. . .
So kneel in prayer in His presence
and you'll find no need to speak,
For softly in silent communion
God grants you the peace that you seek.

HE UNDERSTANDS

Although it sometimes seems to us
our prayers have not been heard,
God always knows our every need
without a single word,
And He will not forsake us
even though the way is steep,
For always He is near to us,
a tender watch to keep. . .
And in good time He will answer us,
and in His love He'll send
Greater things than we have asked
and blessings without end. . .
So though we do not understand
why trouble comes to man,
Can we not be contented
just to know it is God's plan?

I Think of You and
I Pray for You, Too

Often during a busy day
I pause for a minute to silently pray.
I mention the names of those I love
And treasured friends I am fondest of—
For it doesn't matter where we pray
If we honestly mean the words we say,
For God is always listening to hear
The prayers that are made by a heart that's sincere.

BREAKFAST FOR THE SOUL

I meet God in the morning
and go with Him through the day,
Then in the stillness of the night
before sleep comes I pray
That God will just take over
all the problems I couldn't solve,
And in the peacefulness of sleep
my cares will all dissolve.
So when I open up my eyes to greet another day,
I'll find myself renewed in strength
and there will open up a way
To meet what seemed impossible
for me to solve alone,
And once again I'll be assured
I am never on my own.

THE FIRST THING EVERY MORNING
AND THE LAST THING EVERY NIGHT

Were you too busy this morning
to quietly stop and pray?
Did you hurry and drink your coffee
then frantically rush away,
Consoling yourself by saying—
God will always be there
Waiting to hear my petitions,
ready to answer each prayer?
Strength is gained in the morning to
endure the trials of the day
When we visit with God in person
in a quiet and unhurried way,
For only through prayer that's unhurried
can the needs of the day be met,
And only through prayers said at evening
can we sleep without fears or regret.
For all of our errors and failures
that we made in the course of the day
Are freely forgiven at nighttime
when we kneel down and earnestly pray.
So seek the Lord in the morning
and never forget Him at night,
For prayer is an unfailing blessing
that makes every burden seem light.

Now I Lay Me Down to Sleep

I remember so well this prayer I said
Each night as my mother tucked me in bed,
And today this same prayer is still the best way
To sign off with God at the end of the day
And to ask Him your soul to safely keep
As you wearily close your tired eyes in sleep,
Feeling content that the Father above
Will hold you secure in His great arms of love. . .
And having His promise that if ere you wake,
His angels reach down, your sweet soul to take,
Is perfect assurance that, awake or asleep,
God is always right there to tenderly keep
All of His children ever safe in His care,
For God's here and He's there
and He's everywhere. . .
So into His hands each night as I sleep,
I commend my soul for the dear Lord to keep,
Knowing that if my soul should take flight,
It will soar to the land where there is no night.

THE POWER OF PRAYER

I am only a worker employed by the Lord,
And great is my gladness and rich my reward
If I can just spread the wonderful story
That God is the answer to eternal glory. . .
And only the people who read my poems
Can help me to reach more hearts and homes,
Bringing new hope and comfort and cheer,
Telling sad hearts there is nothing to fear,
And what greater joy could there be than to share
The love of God and the power of prayer.

A Prayer of Thanks

Thank You, God, for the beauty
around me everywhere,
The gentle rain and glistening dew,
the sunshine and the air,
The joyous gift of feeling
the soul's soft, whispering voice
That speaks to me from deep within
and makes my heart rejoice.

I COME TO MEET YOU

I come to meet You, God, and as I linger here
I seem to feel You very near.
A rustling leaf, a rolling slope
Speak to my heart of endless hope.
The sun just rising in the sky,
The waking birdlings as they fly,
The grass all wet with morning dew
Are telling me I just met You. . .
And gently thus the day is born
As night gives way to breaking morn,
And once again I've met You, God,
And worshipped on Your holy sod. . .
For who could see the dawn break through
Without a glimpse of heaven and You?
For who but God could make the day
And softly put the night away?

Thank You, God, for Everything

Thank You, God, for everything—
the big things and the small—
For every good gift comes from God,
the giver of them all.
First, thank You for the little things
that often come our way—
The things we take for granted
and don't mention when we pray—
The unexpected courtesy,
the thoughtful, kindly deed,
A hand reached out to help us
in the time of sudden need.
Oh, make us more aware, dear God,
of little daily graces
That come to us with sweet surprise
from never-dreamed-of places.
Then thank You for the miracles
we are much too blind to see,
And give us new awareness
of our many gifts from Thee.
And help us to remember that
the key to life and living
Is to make each prayer a prayer of thanks
and each day a day of thanksgiving.

So Many Reasons to Love the Lord

Thank You, God, for little things
that come unexpectedly
To brighten up a dreary day
that dawned so dismally.
Thank You, God, for sending
a happy thought my way
To blot out my depression on a disappointing day.
Thank You, God, for brushing
the dark clouds from my mind
And leaving only sunshine
and joy of heart behind.
Oh God, the list is endless
of the things to thank You for,
But I take them all for granted
and unconsciously ignore
That everything I think or do,
each movement that I make,
Each measured, rhythmic heartbeat,
each breath of life I take
Is something You have given me
for which there is no way
For me in all my smallness to in any way repay.

GOD, ARE YOU THERE?

I'm way down here—You're way up there.
Are You sure You can hear my faint,
faltering prayer?
For I'm so unsure of just how to pray—
To tell You the truth, God,
I don't know what to say.
I just know I'm lonely and vaguely disturbed,
Bewildered and restless, confused and perturbed,
And they tell me that prayer
helps to quiet the mind
And to unburden the heart, for in stillness we find
A newborn assurance that Someone does care
And Someone does answer
each small, sincere prayer.

GOD'S ASSURANCE
GIVES US ENDURANCE

My blessings are so many,
my troubles are so few—
How can I be discouraged
when I know that I have You?
And I have the sweet assurance
that there's nothing I need fear
If I but keep remembering
I am Yours and You are near.
Help me to endure the storms
that keep raging deep inside me,
And make me more aware each day
that no evil can betide me.
If I remain undaunted though
the billows sweep and roll,
Knowing I have Your assurance,
there's a haven for my soul,
For anything and everything
can somehow be endured
If Your presence is beside me
and lovingly assured.

IT'S ME AGAIN, GOD

Remember me, God? I come every day
Just to talk with You, Lord,
and to learn how to pray.
You make me feel welcome;
You reach out Your hand.
I need never explain, for You understand.
I come to You frightened and burdened with care,
So lonely and lost and so filled with despair,
And suddenly, Lord, I'm no longer afraid—
My burden is lighter and the dark shadows fade.
Oh God, what a comfort to know that You care
And to know when I seek You, You will always be there.

COMMON GROUND

Father, make us kind and wise
So we may come to realize
That God the Father made us all,
The rich, the poor, the great, the small,
And in the Father's holy sight,
No one is yellow, black, or white,
And peace on earth cannot be found
Until we meet on common ground.
Great is our gladness to serve God through others,
For our Father taught us
we are all sisters and brothers.

THIS IS ALL I ASK

Lord, show me the way
I can somehow repay
The blessings You've given to me. . .
Lord, teach me to do
What You most want me to
And to be what You want me to be. . .
I'm unworthy I know
But I do love You so—
I beg You to answer my plea. . .
I've not got much to give
But as long as I live
May I give it completely to Thee!

WELLS OF SALVATION

Oh blessed Father, hear this prayer
And keep us all in Your care.
You are so great. . .we are so small. . .
And when trouble comes as it does to us all
There's so little that we can do
Except to place our trust in You!

So place yourself in His loving care
And He will gladly help you bear
Whatever lies ahead of you.
And God will see you safely through,
For no earthly pain is ever too much
If God bestows His merciful touch.